To My Kids

Juan M. Valenzuela P.

Editor: Kathryn Willms

Front cover image and design: Crista Valenzuela

Issued in print and electronic formats.
ISBN 978-0-578-33965-8 (hardcover)

This is an original print edition of *To My Kids.*

CONTENT

Part II. On Money, Work, and Business

INTRODUCTION

Dear Kids,

I'm turning 50 years old a couple of months from now. As I have told you before, my dad passed away at 51. Although I am not expecting to die at the same age he did, I wanted to mark the occasion by creating something special that might be of some value to you. So I decided to write this book.

In it, you will find my personal philosophy of life and business, broken down into individual pieces of advice. Although each one could be the topic of its own book, I have designed them to be just a few lines long, going directly to the point. I hope this way you can come to me to discuss them over, which I would love to do.

The work is divided in two parts, not because it has to be but because that's how my mind works: recommendations for living a happy life, and advice for success related to work and money. Of course, these absolutely overlap, and sometimes it is difficult to draw a line between them. So you may find useful advice on certain topics in both parts.

You might also notice some redundancies between topics; for instance, there is a lesson on decision making in each part, but each was written with different context in mind.

It is important to note that this work is not attempting to provide universal truths of any kind. It is simply the product of what I have learned being in this world for almost 50 years. You might agree with certain pieces of advice and disagree with others. Either way, as I wrote before, I would love for you to come to me to discuss your thoughts and ideas.

I would recommend reading this book one topic at a time, and using the rest of the day to reflect on that topic. Then you can come back to read the next topic, and so on. There is no hurry; take your time.

I hope you see in this work a reflection of the deep love and pride I have for you kids.

So, here it is, my legacy to you. I hope you find it useful...

Part 1. On Life

1.1. Happiness

Since you were really young, I have often asked you: What is the most important thing in the world (meaning, in life)? You would tell me: "To be happy," to which I would reply: "And how do you achieve happiness?" You would say: "By being the best person I can be." And we stopped there.

Let's get a little deeper into what happiness is and how to become the best version of ourselves.

In my life, I've found that happiness a feeling of satisfaction that emanates from knowing that:

1. We did our best in a given situation, even if the outcome was different than the one we expected.

2. We had a positive impact on another person; in other words, we have made someone's life better by being a part of it. The more people we impact in a positive way, the greater the feeling.
3. We continue to grow in all aspects of our lives: physically, by working out, keeping a balanced diet, and maintaining bodily autonomy; mentally, by continuing to learn new things; and spiritually, by developing new habits, honoring our values, and gaining a better understanding of ourselves.

We can see that these are all things we can control no matter what our life circumstances. They come from within. So we always have the tools to be happy.

1.2.   Love, Forgiveness, and Gratefulness

These three practices are the pillars of almost all religions, and practicing them is a key element to achieving happiness, so let's explore what they mean:

Love

There are several definitions of love, but the one applicable here has to do with having genuine concern for the happiness of others.

When we make a positive impact in another person's life, we help to make his life better. Thus, we help him to become a better person and, in turn, make him happier. If we can do that with every person we meet, we become better people ourselves—and happier ones!

Forgiveness

When someone does something that hurts us, we may feel hatred or resentment towards this person, and these feelings can affect us even more negatively than the original action that hurt us. Even worse, these negative feelings can last for years or even for life.

Negative feelings like hatred or resentment cloud our minds and prevent us from making the right decisions. And when we don't make good decisions, we fail to become the best version of ourselves, which will make us unhappy.

The only way to get rid of these negative feelings is to forgive. Once we forgive, we remove this burden, which allows us to get back on track towards living a happy life.

But there is a warning here: To forgive does NOT mean to forget. When we forgive, we let go of the negative feelings towards the person who hurt us, but we don't forget the experience of being hurt. This way, we retain the important lesson we've learned and don't put ourselves in a position where we could get hurt again in the same way.

Gratefulness

> When you focus on what you lack you lose what you have. When you focus on what you have you get what you lack. – Greg McKeown

At all times, we are blessed with many things. It is important to learn to identify what they are and be grateful for them: food, shelter, family, friends, education, belongings, and so on. For instance, instead of complaining about the traffic, we can choose to be grateful that we have a car.

The real challenge arises when we compare our blessings with somebody else's. This can open the door to feelings of envy and dissatisfaction. Try to avoid comparisons at all costs. The way to do that is to focus on our blessings and to be thankful for them. Also we should try to be thankful for the blessings of others because, in the end, we also want them to be happy. Their happiness should bring us ours.

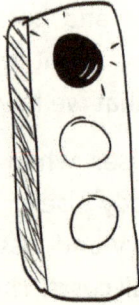

1.3.   Do Not Be Dead Right

Most disagreements among people are about being right; this has led to righteous wars and fights, lost friendships, and new enemies. And at the end of the day, what good has "being right" brought to the life of the victor?

Let's use a hypothetical example: A pedestrian stands at a traffic light, waiting to cross the street. The light turns green, so it is technically his turn to cross. However, a truck is speeding towards the intersection. It's clear that its driver has not seen the light, or he just doesn't care. But the pedestrian thinks: "No way, it is my turn to cross the street. The light is green for me and red for the truck. I'm going!" He was right, and now he is dead.

1.4.   Attitude

Around ten percent of how we do in life depends on the events and opportunities presented to us. The remaining ninety percent depends on how we react to these events and opportunities. So it is not about luck, it is about attitude. If we walk through life with a positive attitude, always willing to make the best of any situation we might encounter, always willing to help others, and always willing to become better versions of ourselves, we will be able to achieve a happy life.

So, we should try not to complain and learn to look at the positive side of the situations in which we find ourselves.

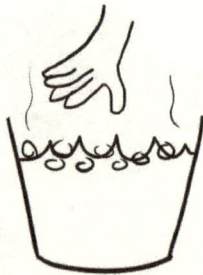

1.5.   Take Responsibility

This point is closely related to the last one ("Attitude").

How many times do we hear people complain about something that has happened to them? I would argue that, in reality, events DON'T just happen to us. They occur because we have placed ourselves in a position where they could happen. Looking at it this way, whatever happens to us is our responsibility. This could be taken as a negative, but I think it is a positive. It means it is our responsibility to put ourselves in positions where good things can happen to us.

Every effect has a cause, so every outcome in our lives is the result of either a decision we made or a position we took. In other words, the only one responsible for what happens to us is ourselves. Understanding this responsibility will drive us to make wiser decisions and to take wiser positions.

1.6.   Never Force Nature

Things have their own perfect nature. People do too. Everything does.

Sometimes, in order to get what we want, we try to force things to change so they fit our desires rather than their natural ways of being. This is a big mistake, and it never works out the way we want.

We must learn to flow with nature. All natural processes have their own timeframe and way of unfolding, which we need to respect to see or receive the intended outcome of a given process.

If we try to force our will, timeframe, rules, etc., on others or the world around us, we are certain to fail. But by identifying, learning, and understanding these natural processes, we can take positions that encourage positive outcomes, and profit from them.

1.7.   Take Care of Yourself

We are our own greatest asset, so it's important to take care of ourselves in three ways: physically, to stay healthy; mentally, to stay lucid; and spiritually, to understand our mission in life.

So, let's explore these three aspects more closely:

Physical Health

There is a big difference between feeding ourselves and eating. When we feed ourselves, we consider not just flavor or desire but what our bodies need. I believe in trying to stay away from sugar, unless it's in its natural form (fruits, etc.), and that we should also avoid fried foods and milk derivatives. Instead, we should try to include vegetables in every meal (or fruits in our breakfast), along with proteins and grains.

Exercising on a daily basis can have incredible benefits, especially if we follow these three rules:

1. Do not get hurt by going beyond our limits.
2. But try to improve and push those limits.
3. Exercise should be fun, so let's choose an activity that we enjoy.

When we feel sick or get injured, it's important to remember that our body has the ability to heal itself. I try to avoid taking medicine or going to a physician unless it is really necessary. Again, we are served best by flowing with nature, not pushing against it.

Mental Health

It's important to learn to face and overcome our fears. Everything we want lays on the other side of them.

We should be aware that our minds tend to exaggerate. Often bad events are not as bad as we visualize them to be.

How many times have you started a task and then found yourself distracted by another? And then a new task interrupts that second task? And another gets in the way of the third? Before long, we've completely forgotten and neglected the task we needed to do in the first place.

I've found that it's often best to focus on doing one thing at a time, staying mentally with it and trying not to think about anything else until it is finished. Multitasking can be hard on our mental health and get in the way of our efficiency.

Also let's stop worrying. If we can control or solve a problem, great, let's do it; if we need to and can ask for help, go for it. We should do whatever is in our power to solve the issues we face, keeping in mind that we want to conform to the flow of nature and not force anything. But there are times when a situation is beyond our control and we can't do anything but wait. When we find ourselves in these moments, we should recognize that we did everything we could, and trust that everything is going to be ok and we will solve the problem in its proper time.

Think about the outcomes of previous situations that felt beyond your control. The outcomes might not have been what you wanted, but they were probably way better than the worst-case scenario you imagined. In the end, trust me, it is ALWAYS going to be fine, so we gain nothing by worrying.

Spiritual Health

I'm not going to get religious here, but I think we are all aware that there is more to us than our minds and bodies, so let's explore spirituality by discussing the concepts of peace and calm.

We all have access to a feeling or state of peace that comes when we know that we are giving our best effort in every aspect of our lives, and that we are growing in every way. To tap into this peace within, we can meditate for at least 10 minutes a day; all we need is to find a comfortable position with our backs straight, clear our minds, and focus on our breath.

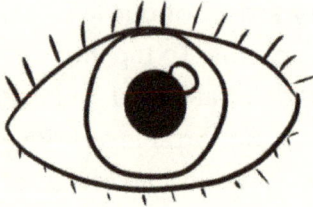

1.8.   How Things Really Are

We cannot see things as they are. No matter how hard we try, our limited experience and our values and prejudices prevent us from seeing the world objectively. So, instead of seeing things as they are, we tend to see them as we are. This is probably the main reason we sometimes do not get the outcomes we expect.

Being aware of this truth can be very helpful when making decisions or when dealing with other people. It makes us humble, which is a good thing because this humility encourages us to listen and to try to understand people with different backgrounds, experiences, and values, which allows us to see a much bigger picture.

1.9.   The World Is as It Is

We tend to think that the world is as we want it to be. We believe we have a clear understanding of how it works. But this is an arrogant assumption, and it can lead us to make wrong decisions and thus fail to achieve our goals.

This is why it is necessary to recognize that the world is how it is, not as we want it to be. And with that recognition, we open ourselves up to learning to understand the nature of things, and to making decisions aligned with that nature, so by cause and effect, we are able to achieve, in a natural way, the outcome we are looking for.

1.10. The Golden Rule

The golden rule, as it is usually explained or described, entreats us to treat others the way we would want to be treated. However, other people are not us, and they may not wish to be treated like us. So, I would suggest the real golden rule should be: Treat others the way they want to be treated. This is significantly harder.

How do we know how they wish to be treated? By asking, listening, and understanding.

There is another way to read the golden rule in a completely different context: Whoever has the gold makes the rule. It is not fair, but let's remember, "the world is as it is."

1.11. On Information

Uncertainty is a constant in life. We can never see the whole picture; nobody can. The universe of what is unknown is far vaster than the universe of what can be known. So we should be aware that most of the time the information we receive is the information the media delivering this information wants us to know.

Once we see the world in this light, it is easy to grasp the importance of never trying too hard to be right. After all, what is "right"? Instead, by flowing with the nature of things, we place ourselves in positions where good things can happen to us.

1.12. Self-Knowledge

So, if we cannot really have knowledge of the external world, can we at least have knowledge about ourselves?

I don't know. Think about the countless times our reactions to a situation are unexpected, even to ourselves. This is why it is said that human behavior is probabilistic, not deterministic. If we always reacted the same way, we would stop being human.

For this reason, it is very important to have a strong set of values to give us direction (values like those discussed in this book).

However, just because self-knowledge might be uncertain does not mean it is not worth trying to get it. At least we know where to look ... within ourselves.

One way to build self-knowledge is through meditation. Stopping our minds while fixing our attention on our breathing for at least fifteen minutes per day can help us keep calm and mindful and develop a deeper understanding of ourselves.

1.13. Practice

Practice leads to mastery. Whatever we want to accomplish, whether it's playing a musical instrument or a sport, learning a craft, doing well at our jobs, or even meditating, we need to practice. Things seldom go right the first time we try them; we need to work hard to achieve the results we are looking for.

In his book *Outliers*, Malcolm Gladwell tells us that it takes 10,000 hours of practice using the correct technique to achieve mastery. Think about it; it takes years.

The trick is to stick with it, find fun in practice, be very patient, and never give up.

We will get there ... eventually!

1.14.   Flying Bumblebees

Once a teacher told me that scientists analyzed the body mass and weight of a bumblebee, and the size of its wings, and they scientifically concluded that the wings are too small for its mass and weight. It shouldn't be possible for the bumblebee to fly; and yet it does.

How? I believe the bumblebee flies because no one has told it that it cannot.

Analogically, we can do anything that we set out to do if we never, ever, let anyone tell us that we can't do it. Remember, things that seem impossible are only impossible until they're done.

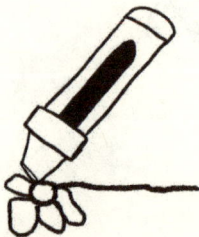

1.15. Never Get Old

I think it was George Bernard Shaw who said: "I did not stop playing because I got old; I got old because I stopped playing."

We should never stop playing, having fun, and finding joy in life. Every chance we get to do something fun, like jumping in a swimming pool, dancing, playing sports, playing music, playing games, etc., we should take it, and experience the joy that comes with it.

It's important to remain young at heart and never stop doing things because they are not appropriate for people "our age."

1.16. Fight Your Ego

There are two big opposing forces that coexist within us. Cartoon artists sometimes visualize them as a little angel and a little devil that sit on our shoulders, giving good and bad advice, and influencing our daily decision making. Let's rename these forces our ego (for the little devil) and our conscience (for the little angel).

Now let's consider the characteristics of the ego (since this is the force we need to fight):

Our ego wants us to think that we are better and more important than others, so we deserve more than them. It encourages us to aspire for external recognition and material possessions we don't really need; it wants us to give into our cravings and the many temptations it promises will bring us physical and psychological pleasure with no effort whatsoever. All we have to do is pay for the things we want and not think of the consequences.

But in the end these things will never fulfill our spirit. How long does the owner of a huge house or a really expensive possession really spend admiring or enjoying it? The answer is, not too long, because things are not that important.

A person should be the master of his things, and when it's otherwise, he starts to see his things as personal idols, and his life becomes miserable.

It's the ego that makes us judge people by their looks and possessions: their clothes, jewelry, the car they drive, the house they live in, their lifestyle in general. But when we realize how stupid this is and that it only leads to our own misery, it's clear that it is better we don't judge, at least not on that basis.

If we are truly looking to find happiness, we must learn how to fight and control our ego, and follow our conscience instead.

1.17. Dealing with Pleasures and Possessions

Let's be clear: pleasure and possessions can be very good things. We deserve them, and we should have and enjoy them.

However, it is important to NEVER depend on them. We rule them. They don't rule us.

When we have pleasures and possessions but understand we really don't need them, we put ourselves in a position where we have nothing to lose. Which is a good thing! It means we know that nothing will happen to us if we suddenly lose everything.

So, if we want to buy that ultra-expensive thing, and we have the means, let's buy it, always remembering that first, it will NOT make us happy, and second, if something bad happens to that new ultra-expensive possession, it won't really matter because it was never that important in the first place. If we cannot have this attitude towards our new possessions, then we should NOT buy them.

One other note on possessions: I believe that we should try to buy only the things we need. By that I mean the things we are going to use on a regular basis. Too much stuff fills the room and give us a sense of disorder.

When we replace something or buy something new, it's nice to get rid of something we no longer need, thus avoiding accumulating stuff.

1.18. On Decision Making

Making decisions while upset is a mistake. When we're emotional, we tend to use our gut instead of our mind to make our decisions, which makes it far more likely we are going to regret them.

We should always try to see the "big picture" and understand the context for the decision we're making.

Then we need to think through the possible outcomes in every time frame: short, mid, and long term.

And finally, and maybe most importantly, proof that we've made the right decision comes from asking ourselves: Will it make me happy?

1.19. Positive Impact

We are responsible for touching and changing the lives of the people we meet in positive ways, in other words, making their lives better, with the knowledge that this is how we become truly happy.

These positive actions can take many forms, and their impact does not necessarily have to be immediate nor physical. Sometimes just planting a seed in another person's mind to help them figure something out on their own is more than enough.

Other times, financial aid is an appropriate form of help. Just keep in mind that the goal is a permanent and life-changing improvement, and financial aid is a short-term help unless you invest in long-term assets such as education.

In order to create that positive impact, the recipient needs to be willing to receive it. Otherwise we're wasting our time. Let's avoid that.

It is very important to teach by example. For instance, extolling on the benefits of working out sounds empty when it comes from a person who does not exercise. As a result, it is less likely to make a positive impact than if the same advice was given by someone who works out every day and is already receiving the benefits of exercise.

1.20.   Trust and Credibility

We must strive to remain trusted and reliable, and the key to that is being 100% honest and straight.

It is important to NEVER lie, even to a small kid or to an elder, and to fulfill our promises, or be accountable when there's some reason we can't.

Our credibility is our biggest asset. Others see us not as we are but as we behave, and trust is hard to earn. We build it over time by constantly delivering and telling the truth no matter what. It is also really easy to lose. It just takes a little lie or an expectation unfulfilled.

Trust and credibility are how we earn one of the best things in life: friendship or good relationships. When we trust and are trusted, we get help from trustworthy people (that is why we trust them). When we are not trustworthy, others take care when dealing with us; they become dubious about our intentions and ability to deliver on our promises. That's a place we do not want to be.

1.21. Taking Life Too Seriously

There's a saying that goes: "Don't take life too seriously, you won't get out of it alive." This is good advice. We should take all the opportunities we get to enjoy life and to have fun in the process. It is important to learn to enjoy what we do; this makes it easy to grow and become a better person, which is what happiness and life are all about.

1.22.   Choosing Your Friends

While being conscious of our responsibility to have a positive impact on most people we meet, we should take particular care when choosing our friends. To paraphrase a well-known saying, gather with millionaires and you will become the next one; gather with athletes and you will become the next one; gather with stupid people and you will become the next one.

This is why it is so important to try to cultivate relationships with people who make us grow, people who have a positive impact on us, people with whom we can have deep conversations and explore the meaning of life, people whom we can easily go to for advice.

At the same time, we should stay away from complainers, negative people, and those who find a problem for every solution. While we want to be a positive force in our interactions with this type of person, I find the best way to avoid being contaminated by negative thoughts is to stay far away from them, and the people who hold them.

1.23. Choosing Your Spouse

This is an important choice in life, and it requires luck, because our spouse needs to choose us too. We need to be mutually chosen. Our choice should be someone we want to spend the rest of our lives making happy, even more than pursuing our own personal happiness. If (it's a big IF) the other person does the same, it's the recipe for a very happy marriage.

So, we need to concern ourselves with two questions: Are we willing to sacrifice our own personal happiness for our spouses' happiness? And are they willing to do the same?

It is also important to choose someone who makes us a better person.

1.24. Choosing a Career

The most common mistake in choosing a field of study at university is focusing on how easy it will make it for us to get a good job and make a lot of money with the knowledge we acquire...

Choosing a field of study really means choosing a specialization. So, it better be something that we really love.

Later on, life will happen and we will end up doing what we do, but at least we will be experts in what we really love.

1.25. Order

We have already reviewed the first step to creating order in our lives: having only the belongings that we need. The second is an easy but tricky one, sometimes more difficult than it looks: having a place to keep every belonging.

When we can achieve this, we will seldom struggle to find our stuff, and our life will look and feel ordered.

And because our inner environment reflects our outer environment, once we do this with our belongings, our mind will automatically follow, becoming ordered and clearer. However, we should also make a conscious effort to do, and think about, only one thing at a time, and avoid passing to the next one until we have finished the first. A to-do list can work. Just keep in mind that unforeseen events happen, and sometimes we need to improvise as we go, so it is important to prioritize.

1.26. Broken Window

When something breaks in our lives, whether it's a physical object, a relationship, or something else, it's important to try to immediately fix it. Otherwise it will keep deteriorating until we have to discard it.

For example: Imagine a nice building. One day, by accident, one of its windows is broken, but no one fixes it. Since no one seems to care enough to fix it, the next week it has ugly graffiti painted on its wall. Now there are two things to fix ... still no one fixes them. The following week, a homeless person sleeps on the floor outside the building and leaves his trash, which no one picks up. Suddenly the nice building is no longer so nice. People are scared to walk close to it. Eventually as it falls into ruin, it becomes the site of criminal and violent acts.

This is why we should fix things the moment we realize they are broken.

1.27. Always Have a Project

In order to stay motivated, it helps to always be working towards a goal: buying a house, saving for something, achieving faster running or swimming times, or whatever milestone we want to set for ourselves.

While it is important to keep in mind really long-term goals, like finding our mission in life (so we can answer yes when we ask ourselves: Are you doing what you came here to do?), these mid-term and short-term milestones will assure us that we are on track for achieving the long-term ones.

Besides, every time we hit a milestone, we get a sense of accomplishment and satisfaction that keeps us going for the next goal, and so on. Setting goals helps us get out of bed in the morning with a sense of purpose and with the right attitude to accomplish whatever we set out to do.

Part II. On Money, Work, and Business

2.1. Money as Poker Chips

Money is a means for acquiring stuff, and we need a certain amount of stuff. Looking at it that way, it's clear we need money to live and often to help others. So while money does not buy happiness or in its own right make us better people, when invested correctly it can help us become better people.

Let's think about money as poker chips; in the game of poker, when we can no longer buy chips, we can no longer play. The same is true of money with one huge difference: we can and will always make more. So let's not look at it as treasure but as means to different ends.

When the time comes to bet our chips (spend or invest our money), we should do it for something we

need, or, even better, something that brings or
could bring us happiness.

2.2.   Every Cent We Spend Casts a Vote

This is so true. When we buy a good or service, we are financing (giving money to) the person or institution who owns the brand, product, or service we are consuming. And by doing so, we are not only sending a message that we support them, we're also enabling them to make and sell more of the same product (or service).

This means that every time we buy something that has been stolen, even if we don't know it is stolen, we are sending a message that we support more thefts. Every time we buy a product or service derived from crime, we are voting for more crime. Every time we buy cheap, low-quality products, we are shouting to the market that we want more cheap, low-quality products to be made. Every time we buy from a street vendor who is blocking the street and who does not pay taxes, we are expressing that we are okay with these actions and incentivizing more vendors like him to do the same.

So, we should choose our purchases wisely, even going so far at times as to assess where a product comes from, its quality, and the kind of company that makes it, to ensure we're supporting the things we believe in.

2.3.   Choices

Sometimes we believe that we have to choose between two unrelated things. For instance, when we are on vacation and we would like to have a massage and also a fancy dinner, but both are kind of expensive, we immediately think that we need to make a decision between them. Most of the time this is false.

We can and should choose both. Not doing so is to limit ourselves, and that is the last thing we want to do. We deserve great things, so we have to aim for greatness.

2.4.   On the Cost of Things

When we evaluate costs, we tend to assess them in terms of the value of the benefit of the good or service being costed to us. Then we compare that to the cost and value of alternative goods or services. Which is fine. But there are times when we might think something we really need costs too much but neglect to see that it is much more expensive NOT to have it. For instance, if you think education is expensive, try ignorance.

This concept is really useful in business. We might be reticent to make an investment that will put us ahead of our competition because it costs too much. But if we do not make it and our competitors do, we could lose an important part of our business.

So, we should always be aware of this real but often hidden cost: the cost of NOT having "it."

2.5.   Working for Money

This is a hard and fast rule for me. We should NEVER work for money. When we do not see a purpose in our work or feel that it's making an impact, we aren't motivated by it, we won't like it, and it will ultimately make us unhappy and fill us with negative feelings. Criminals "work" for money. We should avoid it at all costs.

Let's imagine two construction workers building a wall. When we approach the first one and ask him what he is doing, his reply is "I am pasting bricks." When we approach the second with the same question, his reply is "I am building a cathedral."

Which of them do you think wakes up every morning happy and willing to keep working? Which would do a better job?

We should love what we do and charge accordingly, the more the better, but always understanding why we are doing it. It should never be for the money.

2.6.   Worrying about Money

Here I am going to write from my own experience. I used to worry about having money to pay for school tuitions, vacations, future expenses, and so on.

However, every time we had a big financial commitment, somehow new business would come into my life, giving me the resources to pay for that commitment. This has been a constant my whole life.

So, my own personal conclusion is: if we need more, we only need to work more, and it will come. Let life flow and don't force nature. At the same time there's no need to be suicidal about money and overspend. Prudence is always the best policy.

There is no scientific way to prove my theory, but personal experience has taught me it is not good to worry or fight about money: there is a lot out there, and with the right strategy it will come when we need it.

2.7. Make Big Bets

When we stop worrying about money, we can start getting ready to make big bets. After all, at the end of the day the only thing we have to lose is money.

It is important, though, to have an exit strategy and a safety net in case things do not come out as we expect. In other words, we should always keep some income stream in case we lose our bet.

By making big bets I am referring to taking business opportunities that require big cash investments, or making positive changes in our lives that represent a big financial risk, like quitting our job to start a business.

Let's dream big and take big risks, and never regret having taken them. The regret that comes from not taking risks because of fear will be far greater.

2.8.   Avoid Buying Things We Do Not Need

What happens when we buy stuff we do not need or we are not going to use frequently?

One major consideration is we need to find a place to keep the new stuff, so we do not have to see it all the time. This is key for keeping order and thus, clarity of mind. But what if this requires room we do not have? Then we need to make additional room for our new thing, maybe by getting rid of another belonging we do use, but that would not make sense, right?

Even if we do find a spot for our latest stuff, if we continue to purchase things we do not need, very soon we will run out of space and begin to have to place these items where we can see them all the time, creating some disturbance in our minds. Maybe we decide to rent a warehouse to keep all that stuff, but isn't it a waste of money to rent space for stuff we seldom use? We might as well sell it cheap in a garage sale, but that requires effort and time and makes little compared to what we originally paid. At the end of the day, we have gained nothing.

So, before buying anything we should ask ourselves four questions:

1. Do we really need it?
2. Is it for a one-time use? If so, can we borrow it from a friend?
3. Where are we going to keep it?
4. Will it make us happy?

2.9.   Give Away

We started this book with a definition of happiness, which is to become the best person we can be and make a positive impact on others. Part of doing that is to give to others and get involved in improving other people's lives. There are plenty of opportunities for this, but I think we should start with ones that are closest to us, so we can really see the impact of our help. In other words, we should first help or support, for instance, the poor kids of our city or our neighborhood rather than the ones from really poor countries we might never visit.

When giving money away, it should not be for the recognition but to improve other people's lives. It's a great feeling to help others.

2.10. Work Versus Capital

Whether we are running our own company or partnering with someone on a business venture, we should learn to differentiate the concepts of work and capital.

Work is what we do to achieve the mission of our company or venture: sales, managing, producing, purchasing, negotiating, and so on.

This work should be compensated on a market basis, meaning that we should set ourselves a compensation similar to what it would cost us to hire someone external to do the same job. If we set ourselves a greater salary than what we would pay someone else to do the job, we are risking the financial performance of our company in the mid-term, even if we are the owner of the business.

In contrast, capital is the amount of money we have to invest in our company, and as with every investment, it deserves a return.

We receive the return on our investments in the form of dividends, this is, our share of the profits the company makes every year.

So, when our company does well and makes money, we get to decide how much of that money we are going to reinvest in our company's growth, and how much we are going to withdraw in dividends as a return on our investment.

When a company grows big enough, we have an opportunity to hire someone who can do our work better than us and supervise them, so we no longer need to work for our company and can instead make a living on the return of our equity, releasing our time for new ventures.

2.11. On Tax Strategies

How many times have you heard that there is nothing certain but death and taxes? More certain is the fact that we don't like to pay taxes. So much so that many times I have seen people sacrifice their companies' growth in order to not pay taxes.

One of the most expensive taxes is the one on income (income tax), which is based on the net income a person or company makes in a given year.

From a tax law view, income is revenues (the amount of money the company brings in) minus deductible expenses, which are the expenses needed to run the business. So the more expenses, the less income, and thus, the less tax you need to pay. Right? Right, but it's a huge mistake to think this way. Here's why.

There are only two ways to finance a company's growth: debt and capital.

Debt is money borrowed from a third party. Debt in excess is high risk, so banks are not willing to let companies or people accumulate too much debt. Once a company has reached its debt leverage potential, the only remaining source of growth financing is capital.

Capital is the money we have in the company. It includes our initial investment plus retained earnings (that is, the profits that we decided not to withdraw in dividends). If a company uses tax strategies to avoid profits, we have less retained earnings, which means less capital. So we have no way to finance an expansion of our business. By not paying taxes, we effectively put a cap on the capital needed to grow the company further.

In other words, businesses that don't make enough to pay taxes are NOT good businesses.

This is not to suggest that we must avoid tax strategies at all costs. Tax planning is really important; it allows you to foresee the impact that future taxes will have on cashflow, and remember cash is king (see 2.13.). We just need to be very careful not to go to the extreme of jeopardizing the growth potential of our company because of a tax strategy.

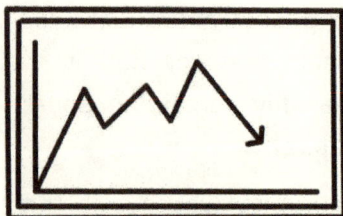

2.12. Recognizing Failure

Sometimes what we thought was a good idea just doesn't work out. Maybe we started a business, but it isn't making money. Worse, it's requiring more and more of our time, effort, and capital. When this happens, if we think there's something we can do differently, we should make the changes fast. But if this does not work, it's best to just recognize our mistake, close the endeavor, learn from the experience, and move on.

In other words: A business that isn't good business should be a closed business.

2.13. Cash Is King

It's important to never, ever, allow our companies to run out of cash. A strong cash position allows us to take advantage of opportunities in the market, to make the investments we need to grow the business, and to run other strategies.

When a company is growing, it requires cash. As our sales increase, we run out of inventory and need to buy more. At the same time, if we give credit to our clients, our accounts receivable increase too (that is, we're waiting to receive more payments from our clients). And we need to keep paying our payroll and operative expenses. This creates a situation where we have less money coming in when we really need it to buy inventory to fill more orders to continue our growth.   So we can only grow as much as our capacity to get additional cash; otherwise we won't be able to meet our financial commitments.

On the other hand, when things are not going well for a business, it will often experience an excess of cash: since sales are low, our purchases decrease, so when we receive pending payments from our clients, the money stays with the company. It's important to be aware of the reason for this excess cash and never take it out of the company, because we will need it when things pick up again.

It is always smart to have an approved line of credit with a bank, but we should only draw from it when we are sure that we will have the resources to pay it back.

2.14. Three Rules of Finance

To keep our companies financially healthy, we should aim to: buy cheap and sell expensive; collect quick and pay slow; and use someone else's money to finance the company. Let's look at them closely:

1. **Buy Cheap and Sell Expensive:** This concept is called margin. When we can add so much value to our goods and services that the market (the people who buy them) is willing to pay way more than what it cost us to provide the goods or services, we make more money from each transaction. And if we can make many transactions with a big margin, we will have placed our company in a position to make a lot of money.

2. **Collect Quick and Pay Slow:** This is how we create liquidity. As mentioned in the previous chapter, when our sales increase, we need more money to produce or get more of what we are selling. A way to break this cycle so we can finance an aggressive increase in sales is to collect fast, meaning to not give credit or payment terms to our clients, or to allow credit or payment terms for only a short period. Also, we should try to do the exact opposite with our suppliers, to pay slow. If we can get payment terms with our suppliers, by the time we need to pay for our orders, we already have those funds collected from our clients. When we are able to achieve both (collect quick and pay slow), our capacity to finance a growth in sales is limitless.

3. **Use Someone Else's Money**: This is how we achieve a great return on investment (ROI).

   Sometimes we need a big amount of money to finance the company's operation. When we can use someone else's money to finance at least part of that operation, the amount of money we need to invest shrinks, and thus, our return on that investment rises. If we can use this money without paying interest, that return will be even greater.

One way to do this is to negotiate credit with a supplier. If a supplier says we don't need to pay her back for 60 days, for that 60 days, she is essentially subsidizing the amount of money we need to put into our business. If we put less money into the business but turn the same profits, we increase our ROI. When the 60 days is up, we pay the supplier out of our profits, but in the meantime, if we've ordered more product from her on 60-day payment terms, we have deferred paying out of pocket and continue to benefit from increased ROI. This cycle can continue indefinitely.

2.15.   Hiring Talent

As with everything cost related, talent is expensive, but it is more expensive not to have it.

The key is to have the right person in the right position.

When hiring, we should look carefully at the candidate and their compatibility with the company's (our) values, principles, and the culture we want to create.

Second, we need to make sure that the candidate has the skills and capabilities to do the job right, and that they have a problem-solving attitude. It's best to stay away from people who find problems with every solution.

Finally, when we find the right person, we should let them do their work, define their desired outcomes, and surprise us with their knowledge and skills. In our relationship with them, we should act more as a mentor or a coach than as a foreman.

For key positions, the best investment we can make is good people, so we should avoid going for the cheapest option and always remember that ordinary people can achieve extraordinary results.

2.16. Taking Positions

As Nassim Taleb explains in his Incerto series, uncertainty is the only constant in life. So the only thing we can do in an uncertain environment is to place ourselves in positions where good things can come to us.

A rising tide lifts all boats, but the ONLY way to benefit from a rising tide is to have a boat.

We cannot win a lottery if we don't have a ticket. Nor can we win at the stock market if we don't have a position, and so on. In life and business, we should always try to take smart positions.

2.17.   Lead by Example

It is really hard to tell people to do something while we are doing the opposite. It sends the wrong signal and confuses others.

What we need to do first is to master the values and attitudes we want to see in others in ourselves. Once we start living them day to day, then, it's time to teach and expect them from others.

This will also accelerate our personal growth and help us to build our own happiness.

2.18.   Order While Working

How clean or messy we keep our working space is an exact reflection of how clean or messy our mind is.

In other words, when there are a ton of papers from different projects on our desk, we encourage our mind to think on all of these different projects at the same time. The problem with this is it makes us lose focus on the task we are doing at any given moment, and as a result, we will probably fail to do it efficiently.

The same thing happens when we open a drawer looking for a file and find a mess. Besides wasting our time finding the file we are looking for, a messy drawer or office numbs the clarity of our thoughts, which we need to execute our projects with excellence.

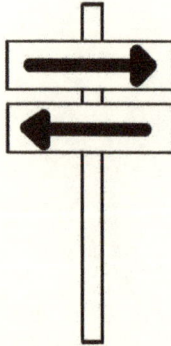

2.19. The Basis of Decision Making

Sometimes people come to us with information, data, and reasons for us to make a decision. They bring us knowledge about something that is happening, and they expect us to make a decision based on that knowledge.

The important thing to understand in these situations is that knowledge is NEVER enough on its own to make an educated or wise decision. In fact, just "knowing" what is going on might lead us to try to force a desired outcome, which may end in a very different result than the one we were aiming for.

We are only ready to make a decision and act on that decision when we really understand the context, causes, and effects of a situation or problem we are approaching—its true nature.

Understanding the problem's nature will allow us to learn how to flow with it until we get it solved.

So, we should try to avoid making a decision based only on information; we should always try to understand the problem before deciding.

We should also beware of what I call "magic words." These are technicalities that we do not understand. Here the advice is easy: If one cannot explain a problem easily, it is because one has not understood it yet (as Albert Einstein said). So if we are asked to make a decision about something we do not clearly understand, it is always better not to decide, and be transparent and honest with whoever is pushing for a decision.

2.20. Build a Framework of Trust

It is easy to work with people we trust.

In order to build a framework of trust, we need to give people freedom but with some boundaries, and those boundaries are the company's values and our personal ones.

When a stakeholder breaches these boundaries, for instance we catch someone telling us a lie, the working relationship should end. Every time we stop trusting somebody, we should also stop working with them—unless we have no choice, but even then, we should quickly try to find a replacement.

When every stakeholder knows this rule, we create an environment of trust within the company, and it will be very easy to work in it.

2.21. Overdeliver

Let's be sure not to create expectations we can't meet. Because no matter how hard we try, we create disappointment when others expect more than what they get.

We should, instead, set the expectations of what we think we can do a little bit lower, and surprise our clients and stakeholders in a positive way. But let's just be smart enough to avoid setting the bar too low.

AFTERWORD

Is this all? I don't think so. It is all I can remember right now, but we could add new chapters every now and then, when we find something useful that is worth putting in this work.

I think life is about balance, and as long as we can achieve improvements in every facet of our life, little by little, we will be building the happy life we aspire to live. Please enjoy the journey, because it is here to be enjoyed.

When I think of the source of the content I shared in this work, I realize that most of it was acquired during the last 20 years and has come from multiple sources that I want to thank and recognize.

First thanks to Gaby, my wife (your mom), whose love, positivity, and support have always kept me going. And thanks to you kids for inspiring me to do this work. Also, to Crista, my oldest daughter, who helped me with the amazing art in this book.

Then, to my mentors and friends:

Thank you, Paolo Melloni, Sergio Raimond (RIP), Antonio Grandío, Agustín Galindo, Antonio Siqueiros, Rodolfo Ramírez, Carlos Martínez P, and all of those whose teachings either in our conversations or by example have helped me to become a better person.

Lastly to my authors, the ones whose books I have read and learned from. Sometimes we think we don't remember what a certain book was about, but I believe we always carry some of the ideas with us. Some books you might not even like, but yet a single sentence can have a deep impact in your life. So, thank you, Nassim Taleb, Mark Manson, Daniel Kahneman, Aristotle, Cervantes, Dalai Lama, Malcolm Gladwell, Miguel Angel Dominguez, Aaron Alexander, Richard Bolles, Hal Elrod, Erik Qualman, Richard Thaler, Matt Ridley, Jim Collins, Tom Morris, Ryan Holiday, Adam Grant, Helen Schucman, T. Harv Eker, among many others.

www.ingramcontent.com/pod-product-compliance
Lightning Source LLC
Chambersburg PA
CBHW031928090426
42811CB00002B/116